Julia Davenport is a freelance poet and author. Born into a working-class family in Salford in 1977, she is the youngest of 4 siblings with 2 older sisters and an older brother. She now lives in North Manchester with her mum, stepdad, brother, and cat. Julia holds a BA(Hons) English Language and Literature degree, and she is currently studying for a MA in Creative Writing with The Open University.

Since 2010 her work has been widely published in many poetry anthologies, magazines and exhibitions, and she regularly performs her poetry in bars, pubs, theatres, museums and libraries. She likes to write about anything and everything, but is mainly interested in using poetry as a form of protest, to encourage people to see the world from a different perspective, and to stand up to all forms of injustice.

Julia Davenport is a Survivor of Child abuse, Bullying, and Domestic Violence.

# Order & Chaos

*a collection of protest poems*

## Julia Davenport

Ragiel & Gill Press

Published in 2017
by Ragiel & Gill Press

ISBN 978-0-9955685-2-5

Cover image courtesy of Stuart Miles
at FreeDigitalPhotos.net

Design by Flapjack Press
flapjackpress.co.uk

Printed by Imprint Digital
Upton Pyne, Exeter, Devon
imprintdigital.com

This book is dedicated to my parents Josie and Jeff, who encouraged me to fall in love with books from an early age.
Many thanks to you both for your amazing love and support.

X x x X x x X

---

Special thanks to The University of Manchester, The Manchester Museum, The Open University, Bournemouth University, Cartwheel Arts, Chanje Kunda, Kooj Chuhan, Sea Phensadsaeng, Vicky Foster, Suzie Tubby, Cathy Crabb, Michelle Hughes, Naomi Sumner Chan, Sarah Woodward, Lillian Nevins, Cathy Bryant, Terry Hughes, Ted Badger, The Nubian Times, Sabrina Aziz and the Mind Membership team, Paul Neads at Flapjack Press, Robert Davenport, Michael Angel, and Mr & Mrs Ragiel.

# Contents

Some of these poems first appeared in the following collections and shows:

'Bipolar - Type II' was first published in the mental health charity magazine *Mind Membership News*, issue 29, Autumn 2017.

'Chained' was first published in *Lucidity Poetry Journal International*, vol. 30, issue 3, 2016.

'Soundscapes' was commissioned by Sea Phensadsaeng for BIRSt (Bournemouth University Internet Radio) and first broadcast on 3rd March 2012.

'Shutdown' first appeared in *Lucidity Poetry Journal International*, vol. 31, issue 4, 2017.

'Beauty is a Rainbow' first appeared in *Scribble Magazine* issue 17, published by Cartwheel Arts, 2013.

'Happiness' was first published in *Lucidity Poetry Journal International*, vol. 30, issue 4, 2016.

'ConDem(n) and Resist' first appeared in *Scribble Magazine* issue 15, published by Cartwheel Arts, 2012.

'Salve A Amazonia (Save the Amazon)' first appeared in a multimedia and interactive digital art installation and film called *Chamada from Chico Mendes* by Kooj Chuhan in 2015 (first exhibited at Global Grooves Carnival Arts Centre from 28th February - 21st March 2015), and has since toured many Art and Exhibition Centres throughout the UK.

'Taken for Granted', 'Crystal Clear' and 'Money Talks' first appeared in the poetry anthology *Integrated Inspiration* (ed. Chanje Kunda), published by The University of Manchester, 2010. 'Taken for Granted' and 'Crystal Clear' also featured in exhibitions at the Manchester Royal Infirmary Hospital and The Manchester Museum between October 2010 and January 2011.

My sister was never backward in being forward, so to speak. The loudest voice at the dinner table and often being told off for swearing, clearly indicated an individual at one with voicing her true feelings. On a personal level, reading her poetry can be a bitter sweet experience - bitter due to the painful evocation of childhood memory and sweet - in the sense of pride a big sister (me) can have, when marvelling at her ability to approach the past with such direct and brutally honest defiance. When fuelled by truth, poetry can present itself at its most vital, even when it may expose us to a source of pain. Julia's ability to do this within her own work not only gives voice to past repression but a courageous insight into confrontation. Poems like 'Lost Cause' and 'Black, White and Blue' amplify a refusal to bury abuse by vocally not letting anyone off the hook.

Whilst 'Soul Mate' and 'Soundscapes' reminds us of the happiness which lies in the simplicity of falling in love or listening to music, 'Happiness' reminds us that this much sought-after mental state often lies within us all.

*Order & Chaos* is an attempt to comment on the chaos of life, whilst giving the reader a chance to reflect on the redeeming balance of speaking the truth.

M.J. Hughes

Order & Chaos

## Bipolar - Type II

When I'm hypomanic high
I taste the world like a child,
All sights, smells and sounds fill me up.
I see the world like a brand new place,
Where anything is possible,
Can't sit still, can't relax
With restless palpitations
And panic attacks.
I'm overdosed with adrenaline filled veins,
Up and down the rooms I pace, and I pace,
My mind is racing with great ideas,
But my hands are shaking
And full of fear.
Everything is louder, brighter, more pungent,
Like I've never seen the world before,
Not this way.
Then on a low day I wake up
Traumatised by a horrific nightmare.
I wake up and feel disappointed that I'm still alive.
I hate myself,
I hate how I look,
I hate my life,
I hate my weight,
On low days I wanna be anyone but me,
Cos the voices in my head are mean,
They cut through my self esteem
And make my head and heart ache,
They blame me for all the bad decisions,
And say things like why didn't you just stay with Ian,
Then you never would have met those two abusers you loser,

Then by now maybe, you'd be married and have babies.
All the achievements and good memories are lost
And forgotten like suicidal lemmings jumping off a cliff,
They just can't help themselves.
I feel sick and shaky,
Frustrated and teary eyed,
At this point I can't handle the flashbacks anymore
So I start to depersonalise,
Deep anger and sadness flood out of me
And myself I don't recognise,
And I'm so touchy and defensive
That I can't stop ranting for an hour,
To my mum this is not a surprise,
She understands and forgives me every time,
My psychiatrist says it's not good but I can't help it,
The cause is repressed anger
From an abusive life
And broken childhood.
But don't feel sorry for me,
I'm not the only one who suffers,
I just want you to understand
That when I go manic weird and out of character,
It's not intentional and it wasn't planned.

Do you remember the time when you were five
And you had that nightmare while awake?
While getting dressed for school
A woman appeared in your room,
With blue skin and purple hair
Wearing a silver sequinned dress with boots,
And sat on a golden broom.
She looked like a sophisticated witch or a futuristic alien
From the sixth dimension, subterranean.
She spoke for five minutes in grand telepathic images,
And got frustrated when you didn't understand.
Then she disappeared into a smoky round portal,
And a python appeared where she'd been standing.
It was massive in length
And wider than 3 pairs of giant sized shoes.
The serpent slithered swiftly towards you,
Hissed and spat out its long reptilian tongue.
You ran round the beds then out the bedroom door,
You ran downstairs faster than you ever did before.
Dad was downstairs in the dining room,
Bottles of beer were scattered on the floor.
He staggered towards the kitchen.
I was scared and crying and trying to tell him about my
    nightmare,
But he didn't care, he was angry and lifted me into the air
By picking me up by my ponytailed hair.
Then he began to hit my legs for ages, slapping and punching
Until they bruised, until I stopped crying.
My legs were so purple that mum kept me off school,
I had P.E. that day and she was afraid the teachers would see

And I'd get taken away - into Care.
Do you remember that day?
I wish I could forget that day.
The day I had two nightmares while awake,
The day I had two nightmares in one day.

Heart drained,
Tear stained dress,
No more energy left,
For his negative-ness.

The sociopathic sculptor chisels and chips away
At all your parts,
Personality,
Beliefs,
The way you walk, talk, eat,
Every bit of you,
Until he's chiselled and carved you into the puppet doll
He wants you to be.

Pygmalion is his forgotten ancestor,
A story packaged in linguistics and made tame for Hollywood,
Mr. Sociopath is a modern and morbid version
Of a misguided Ovid,
In other words he's a control freak,
With or without knowing it.

Tried to chip, chip, chip away at my sense of self,
My dreams and goals,
To stay with him means I disappear,
Become a shadow to his ego.

He wants me to love him,
But his words are weapons that wound and crush my soul,
His words are vitriolic verbs,
That slice and dice and niggle at my nerves.

This is war against personae,
Individualism,
Self-image,
All under attack from all angles everywhere,
My defences are battered and broken and worn threadbare.

My energy to stand trial and defend
Needs a rest,
A refuge from the verbal bullets and bombs,
From his venomous fangs and evil spitting tongue.

This car crash love is now in the past,
And can be crushed at the scrapyard at last,
His Eliza Doolittle I could never be,
I much prefer Antigone,
Because I'd rather die a slave,
Than live with him Unfree.

# Chained

I long for the day when I'm free,
The day when these chains lose their grip,
Only then, can I be me.

I wish I could be tied to a tree,
At least there's a chance the rope would slip,
I long for the day when I'm free.

Without him I could just be,
Free from another busted lip,
Only then, can I be me.

I'll sneak out the back and leave my key,
Then he can't give me any gyp,
I long for the day when I'm free.

I know he won't ever agree,
He's a bad habit attached to my hip,
I long for the day when I'm free,
Only then, can I be me.

You kicked my father's soul to the sky,
You sliced and maimed my personality,
You laughed in court at the reasons why,
You drip-drained my brain and identity.

You sliced and maimed my personality,
You ate my heart and spat out my mind,
You drip-drained my brain and identity,
Broke spirits to pieces and stole eyes from the blind.

You ate my heart and spat out my mind,
You are the flashback, the nightmare, the PTSD,
Broke spirits to pieces and stole eyes from the blind,
Now you're the caged demon dying to fly free.

You are the flashback, the nightmare, the PTSD,
You laughed in court at the reasons why,
Now you're the caged demon dying to fly free,
But you kicked my father's soul to the sky.

Androgyny has never been a stranger to me,
As a girl I was just as happy with He-Man as Barbie.
I played with dolls and I played with cars,
I liked wearing vests and I liked wearing bras.
They say women are from Venus and men are from Mars,
But what if you are a bit of both;
Best of Both fluid sliced like Kingsmill 50/50 bread,
How should I speak, act, dress?
When shopping it's always been two pairs of shoes,
One pair pink, and one blue.
We get called lazy, 'just make up your mind',
We get called names unkind; like greedy and oversexed,
But it's not just about sex, or how much you get.
People have views they like to voice,
They tell me to choose,
But it's not a choice.
It's like food;
When you like something, you like it, but can you ever
    really explain why,
Apart from uttering 'it looks/smells/tastes nice'?
Have you ever wondered why does it look/smell/taste nice?
Which part of your brain decides what you do and don't like?
Eyes, nose, taste buds are only part of the equation as they
Filter messages on route to your brain.
What if the subconscious mind is pre-programmed before
    we are born?
The Aura reading said I was exactly in the middle between
    male and female,
The reader said we don't see that very often,
People are usually either mostly female or mostly male.

If we can't choose our favourite foods,
How can we choose who we're attracted to?
What if we love melons and peaches as much as
We love meat and two vegetables?
Are you gonna tell us our taste buds are wrong?
To summarize from a Lady Gaga song:
'We don't care what you say; and
They don't care what you say,
We're on the right track baby,
We were born this way'!!

For I will consider: how you were,
For I will consider: forgiveness,
For I will consider: maybe your childhood was bad,
For I will consider: I gave you many chances,
For I will consider: you were ok at first,
For I will consider: you were tight with your feelings,
For I will consider: you may have mental problems,
For I will consider: you are ill,
For I will consider: you are an alcoholic,
For I will consider: you won't seek help,
So therefore I consider you a lost cause.

## Reciprocate

The aroma is supposed to be like roses,
Flavour like hot chocolate waffles at Blackpool,
Images of hearts on cards for fools,
Blood feelings like music and fire, hidden beneath your skin
    and clothes.

Sparks dance and dart between heads and toes,
A subjective emotion without rules,
A lesson that I missed at school,
The lovers I lost I never chose.

I don't know what I'm doing wrong,
Nails in my heart rip, sting and smart,
I choked on the salt tears buried in my throat.

But I read the book and heard the song,
That didn't help me - romanticised art,
Love is a myth that exists in the mist of the dark water harbour
    with rotted boats.

What is music?
Its mystical power will transform
Like the pendulum voiced hypnotist.
Songs evoke Polaroid photos mind trapped.
Music to dance to
Egyptian Sand dance, Chinese Lion dance, Indian Bhangra,
And Indonesian Balinese. Music to sing to
Love songs that hug you
While Football chants fuel you.
Music to make love to
'Sexual Healing'
Will entice and seduce you.
Music to protest to
Dylan and Marley's rage against racism
Like Political movements moving mountains
With musical mindfulness.
Music to cry to
Rhythmic, harmonic, melodic Blues
Empathise when the world caves in on you.
Music to boost you
Like 'I will survive'
When a lover has left you.
Music to chill to
New Age sounds of birdsong and
Waves to still the mind to.
Music to marry and
Wedding March down the aisle to.
Music to be born to
'Happy Birthday'
To dance down the love canal to.

Music to be buried to
Gregorian chants
Move your soul to heaven
As the angels guide you.
Music to be downloaded to iPods
Like black magic boxes
Holding music makers captive in digitised prisons;
Hip hop DJs scratching and rapping in my ears so clear,
And B-Boys breakdance mind pictures of yester year.
Sound and music is all around,
The soundtrack to life.
So live, love and listen to the sound.

## Shutdown

Numb my heart,
Lobotomise bad memories,
Freeze sexual desire,
Swallow feelings down and push,
Push them right down,
Eat and digest them,
Switch off the mind to them,
Sit on them,
Excrete them,
Shit them out.
Do we really 'fall' in love?
Or do we love because we 'choose' to?

## Soul Mate

Love like electricity does exist,
It charges the heart with power,
It's not a myth in a hazy mist,
It's the queen bee that blooms the smallest flower.

It charges the heart with power,
Lightning bolts dart within the chest,
It's the queen bee that blooms the smallest flower,
It hears your worsts but cheers your bests.

Lightning bolts bolting around the chest,
Values and interests are shared like the bed,
It blinkers your worsts but spotlights your bests,
Warm tingles will swim in your veins, heart and head.

Values and interests are shared like the bed,
It's not a myth in a hazy mist,
Hot tingles will swim in your veins, heart and head.
Love like electricity does exist.

## Sibling Rivalry

I.

My sister is a nerd,
She spends hours chatting online,
Another sheep from another herd,
She doesn't phone she hasn't got time.
Online networking is her thing,
She really can't live without it,
She thinks she's got 500 true friends,
Somehow I very much doubt it.
Her status should be liked, poked, commented upon,
Otherwise she feels let down,
Like a clown with tsunami tears
When there's no one around.
She sends virtual gifts and plays long distance games,
Uses fake profile photos and alias names,
My sister is daft; she gives out too much information,
Damages her eyes and fry's her brain
With constant computer radiation.
The network has consumed her soul,
Infected her heart and
Infested her veins.

II.

My brother is an anomaly,
On most things he's very bright,
But he fears dependence on technology,
And thinks it's something we should fight.
Like a Luddite he refuses to change,
Nostalgic memories smashing machines,

Society he wants to re-arrange,
With anti-capitalist ways and means.
His conspiracy theories drive me mad,
Not everyone on the internet is bad,
Not everyone is trying to steal your identity,
And as for friends I've got plenty.
My brother can't see the good that it does,
It can lead you to friendship and lead you to love,
It helps you contact family
You thought were lost forever.
But my brother won't listen to me,
So I just say "whatever!"

# Gangster Street

*A True Story*

Outside our door on Gangster Street
Is where joyriders and drug dealers meet,
Every night they can be seen
Stealing cars and selling Es,
Graffiti-ing on houses
And robbing local shops,
But the thing is if you call the cops
They run off and hide like dickheads,
And come back when it's late and you're asleep in bed,
They find the biggest bricks to smash your windows in,
They really are a bunch of shits,
They talk tough when they're with their gang,
But on their own they never stand,
Cowards by any other name,
Bullies, cowards, gangsters,
They're all the same,
Vibrating in a sociopathic frequency and feeling no shame,
They've stolen 3 of my sister's cars,
Robbed the newsagent,
Stabbed the off-licence assistant who died from her scars,
Terrorising people they seem to love it,
Act like they can't get enough of it,
One Bonfire Night they left my family a treat,
They set fire to our backyard door,
The fucking freaks,
Another time I came home from school for lunch,
To find they'd sent me something extra to munch,
A 2lb pound rock through the window just missed my head,
I screamed so loud the windows bled,

They even shot a man dead behind our house,
It sounded like giant fireworks when the bullets rang out,
I often wondered why they did it,
And came to the conclusion that some people are just shits.

# Dog Walk

Down the hill me and Charlie walked,
Above us we saw a multitude of wind turbines
Whiter than milk
Dancing on the Pennines,
Car fumes make us cough, cough, cough,
So we stop outside the video shop,
Then Charlie swiftly started to do his business,
Luckily depositing it behind a large bush,
So the manager didn't see or cause a fuss,
Past the kitchen shop
We cross three sets of lights,
Impatient drivers huff, stare and tut
And give us dirty looks,
As though we're trespassing on their roads,
We cross and walk through invisible barricades
Devised by narrow minds.
Past the smell of laundrette and petrol station,
Until Charlie victoriously marks his territory
The Coronation park wall with his noisy urination,
It's 90F degrees so we stop and drink water by the wide
    trunked trees,
Trees create calmness,
Breathing everyone for all time selflessly,
Feeding our lungs,
Does their unselfish existence bring them happiness through
    purpose?
Sniff; sniff every spray Charlie must sniff
And pee over like a competitive graffiti artist,
On we go up Radcliffe New Road,
It's scorching hot but people are out,

Builders are crafting concrete in rotating barrels,
Pavements are steamrolled by men with stressed faces,
New parents walk happily with their babies in prams
To the heart beat of contentment,
My ears are vibrating to the buzz of cyclists, motorbikes,
Fast cars and vans,
Every so often we glimpse a jogger, power walker, pub,
New restaurant, and new houses being built,
We cross over the road to avoid my old life,
The long lane of Lily Hill Street that once led
To the nightmare of the living death.
We turn right at the next set of lights,
We breathe sighs of relief,
That I survived that existence,
That I escaped so sweet,
He said "if you tell I will kill you and all your family".
Many times he nearly killed me,
He killed the old me that I used to be.
Past the Indian restaurant,
We pass what used to be the Bull's Head Pub,
Suddenly my head is filled with the memory
Of being age 23 with old friends and
Singing 'Bohemian Rhapsody' on Karaoke,
For a laugh purposely in the wrong key,
We pass Morrison's and Tandra Taxis,
Then we turn right onto Ringley Road,
The road where the rich people live,
Builders and strangers stare at me,
An RSPCA fundraiser walks by and says "hello"
As if he knows me,
A few minutes later a rich looking man pulls his pedigree
Out of the way and waits for us to pass,
I say "thanks" as we walk by but Charlie decides to try and

Kick-off with the rich man's dog,
I manage to drag Charlie away and I feign
Slight embarrassment, although I'm secretly pleased
With my dog because even though he's mixed breed,
He refuses to hide his anger against human prejudice of dog
    breeds,
We pass the last of the rich houses at last,
And the luxury flats on the left
Those always seem to be empty?

Then we walk down a narrow country lane
With the golf course on the right disguised with barbed fences,
And the farm on the left with black and white sheep
Drinking water from small ponds,
We walk on the right but wish to walk on the left,
But we can't because the path is so narrow
That it fades into nothingness,
The round bushy trees dazzle with their domineering darkness,
The perfect contrast to sun bleached oak leaves and grass of
Hay-like yellow and pastoral greens,
Pastel hues are suddenly dyed,
When the golden sun shines
And reflects light from the roses and carnations nearby,
Now the field is aglow like Rose quartz pink
And purple Amethyst against the light blue inky sky.
Round the last corner and down the hill,
Onto our Avenue and we're home again.
Our walk from Radcliffe to Whitefield and back
Took 1hr and 10 mins,
And although tiring,
I'd do it again; it's more interesting than ironing.

What would you do with 330,000 litres of water?
I'd commission the design of a giant waterwheel
To generate electricity to light up the water
Of the Manchester Ship Canal,
So that Martians flying over Manchester in the dark
Will have a lit up landmark to guide them
On their way to Peel Park,
Make it a source of fuel for cars; send some in a rocket to Mars,
Build a pipeline of water to Africa;
Add some to pesto with paprika,
Take it out, filter it and add some gin,
The taste will make your taste buds grin,
Heat it with solar panels when winter sets in,
Fill with blocks of ice to chill it in summer,
During draughts pray for cloud and rain
(The Canal's lifeblood mother),
Canals are the old veins of every city,
The Factory and Mill's functional forgotten friends,
Watch the water go up and down and round the bends,
Next time you ride the canal by footpath or canal boat,
Listen for the footsteps and echoes,
Look out for the shadows and ghosts of men and horses
Who towed canal boats.
We should remember those who towed the boats,
From Land's End to John O'Groats.

Beauty is: experiencing the excited jumping of a child
waiting for Christmas.

Beauty is: a private joke told by the eyes and laughter of
lifelong friends.

Beauty is: the 10 year old black and white cat who snuggles
up to you and purrs whenever you feel ill or down.

Beauty is: the 100 year old tree in the park housing chirping
love birds, fast moving squirrels, and feeding our lungs.

Beauty is: realising that being is as important as doing.

Beauty is: learning that to forgive is to rise above evil, and is
better than living weighed down by an iron heart full of hate.

Beauty is: seeing a sunset paint fields and highlight the trees.

Beauty is: finally hearing a daughter's laughter after seeing
her so sad for so long.

Beauty is: loving yourself no matter what, loving yourself no
matter how many cynics try to kill your spirit.

## I Lost My Mind

I lost my mind and found a new one,
I lost my ego and found spirit,
I lost my fears and found belief,
I lost the bad people and found self-esteem,
I lost control of my nerves and found enlightenment,
I lost my mind and found transformation,
I lost my mind and found the divine,
I lost my mind and I was reborn,
I lost my mind and found a new one.

# Happiness

She didn't know who she was any more;
Her life was getting harder to swallow.
She was going to find it on another shore;
With a new set of lifelines to follow.

She dug to find it at Cripple Creek;
Scaled 300 steps at Seven Falls.
Rode train to view it from top of Pike's Peak;
And at Edinburgh Castle she inspected the wall.

She walked across the rope bridge at Carrick-a-Rede;
At Garden of the Gods she posed with Balanced Rock.
But to her dismay she didn't succeed;
So returned to her birthplace to take stock.

Mum said: "Achieved what you sought to find?"
I said: "Yes, happiness. But it's inside my mind."

Over 70 years ago today,
Thousands of soldiers threw themselves into the fray,
Those who died were young and old,
Brave and bold,
All someone's sweetheart or someone's son,
Those who survived were the lucky ones,
How did they cope in trenches?
How do you keep your mind sane?
Can you imagine it, living and fighting night and day?
Amongst the noise of incessant bombs and gun fire,
The sea of blood, the cold, the rain, the tears, the pain?
Torn flesh and limbs sit on and just beyond the barbed wire,
Your best friend is lying on the floor behind you dying,
He was shot multiple times in the chest,
Your Stepson Randolph was exploded by a mine,
Grandad Joseph was lucky that a bullet only skimmed
The hat on his head,
Can you imagine instead of your comfy warm bed,
You had to sleep on mud and rain,
And blood and amongst the dead?

# ConDem(n) and Resist

I.

School was Westminster and Eton,
University was Cambridge and Oxford,
Our intelligence and charm cannot be beaten,
Our cunning like cats embarrasses the craftiest fox.
Married with children and in our forties,
Our pastimes are riding and shooting,
Born in Buckinghamshire, Home Counties,
Labour we think needs uprooting.
We and our friends are millionaires,
Old Etonians are the front bench,
Funded by taxes and billionaires,
The Duck House was a small expense.
But we will forge the seas and stormy weather,
Because we are all in this together.

II.

We are the ones you made redundant,
Men with axes let us fall,
We are the ones made homeless, not prosperous,
My income has shrunken to smaller than small.
Men with axes let us fall,
Greedy Bankers; the suited vulture,
My income has shrunken to smaller than small,
Bankers birthed recession with hedge-fund culture.
Greedy Bankers; the suited vulture,
MPs your money feeds you sunny weather,
Bankers birthed recession with hedge-fund culture,
So 'We' are 'Not' in this together.

MPs your money feeds you sunny weather,
We are the ones you made homeless, not prosperous,
So 'We' are 'Not' in this together,
We are the ones you made redundant.

Billions to bail out Banks,
Millions for their Wars,
They spend more on death than they do on life,
Tax Breaks for the rich,
And Bedroom Tax for you,
Tax dodging by monstrous Corporations,
And Benefit Sanctions for you,
House flippin' and expense claims ego trippin' for MPs,
And Food Banks for you,
Tax Breaks for the rich,
And Benefits stopped for you,
Tax Breaks for the rich,
And Credit cards for you,
Tax Breaks for the rich,
And Amigo Loans for you,
Tax Breaks for the rich,
And debts piling up for you.

Tax Breaks for the rich,
But Bankruptcy for you?
Tax Breaks for the rich,
But Food Banks for you?
Tax Breaks for the rich,
But Homelessness for you?
Tax Breaks for the rich,
But Suicide for you?

Here's an equation for you:
Tax Breaks for the rich + Economic Recession
= Austerity is a lie!

AUSTERITY IS A LIE!!!!

They sow seeds of greed
That make the vulnerable bleed,
So they can succeed;
Kissing the arses of corporations,
They suck the dicks of the rich for tainted donations.

How many tax breaks can they give to rich dicks
Who don't need them?
How many ill and disabled people
Can they get away with sanctioning
Lives and benefits away from?

They made you think shopping, films and TV
Were your main life priority,
To keep you distracted from their Wars and Austerity,
They made laws to steal your online privacy
And destroy our civil liberties.
What's it gonna take for you to stand up against inequality?
What's it gonna take for you to stand up for our humanity?
What's it gonna take for you to fight back?

## Money Talks

Some have too much
Some too little
"It makes the world go round"?
"It's the root of all evil"?

The silence is deafening,
The lack of action from governments is deafening,
The stream of people in exodus from Syria is overwhelming
And seems eternal.
Boat people are drowning,
Children are drowning,
Refugee camp people are drowning in their tears and disease.
People trapped in limbo Hell of refugee camps
With man-made wire borders,
Borders lined with 21st Century tents and Refugees,
Sinking in the rain,
Crying in the rain,
And dying in the rain.

## Salve A Amazonia (Save the Amazon)

*The Spirit of Chico Mendes*


He started work at age 9 as a Rubber Tree Tapper,
Working and living in the Amazon Rainforest for 28 years,
The trees were his livelihood, his lifeblood, his friends,
Like mothers giving milk again and again,
Rubber trees dripping white latex from their full trunk breasts.

Amazonia is home to half the world's species,
She births Rubber trees, Nut trees,
And medicinal trees,
A quarter of the world's medicines are from Amazon trees.

1% of landowners own 45% of the forest,
Saying they clear it for Cattle Ranching,
This means they burn it and they log it,
They don't replenish or replant it,
But they deforest and destroy it.

> *The peo-ple, uni-ted,*
> *will ne-ver be de-feat-ed.*

Ranchers expelled 100,000 Tappers from the forest,
Then Tappers had to work for rich landowners,
Were paid low wages and exploited.

> *The peo-ple, uni-ted,*
> *will ne-ver be de-feat-ed.*

> *The peo-ple, uni-ted,*
> *will ne-ver be de-feat-ed.*

Ranchers tried to cut down preserved parts of the forest,
Chico Mendes rebelled and rallied Tappers to protest,
Whole families joined hands to block bulldozers and chainsaws,
They got the UN to listen and create new environmental laws,
Mendes couldn't stand by and let Ranchers kill his
Amazonia Mother for profit,
Instead he stood up against the establishment and he rocked it.

*The peo-ple, uni-ted,*
*will ne-ver be de-feat-ed.*

*The peo-ple, uni-ted,*
*will ne-ver be de-feat-ed.*

*The peo-ple, uni-ted,*
*will ne-ver be de-feat-ed.*

The UN awarded Mendes the Global Environmental 500 Honor,
Then the international communities' ears burned, pricked up,
And listened,
The world opened its eyes and woke up in shock
From its ignorant slumber,
The world Learned new concepts of Deforestation
And Global Warming,
Learned that Mendes' knowledge of the forest
Was a time bomb warning,
Learned that the Amazon Rainforest
Is a provider and a Mother.

*The peo-ple, uni-ted,*
*will ne-ver be de-feat-ed.*

*The peo-ple, uni-ted,*
*will ne-ver be de-feat-ed.*

*The peo-ple, uni-ted,*
*will ne-ver be de-feat-ed.*

Ranchers despised Mendes' Press attention,
And decided to stage an intervention,
By buying all the local press and prohibiting stories
Being run about Mendes,
Like a childish Ranchers biased protest.

*The peo-ple, uni-ted,*
*will ne-ver be de-feat-ed.*

*The peo-ple, uni-ted,*
*will ne-ver be de-feat-ed.*

*The peo-ple, uni-ted,*
*will ne-ver be de-feat-ed.*

Mendes' protests won him Amazon nature preserves, awards,
And attention from the Press,
But with all his achieved success,
He also received constant death threats,
Those who sent them he could easily guess.

*The peo-ple, uni-ted,*
*will ne-ver be de-feat-ed.*

*The peo-ple, uni-ted,*
*will ne-ver be de-feat-ed.*

*The peo-ple, uni-ted,*
*will ne-ver be de-feat-ed.*

On 22nd December 1988 Chico Mendes was murdered,
Shot dead,
While having a shower outside his house,
He was shot in the back of the head,
The Ranchers Darcy and Oloci Alves da Silva
Were found guilty of his death.

*The peo-ple, uni-ted,*
*will ne-ver be de-feat-ed.*

*The peo-ple, uni-ted,*
*will ne-ver be de-feat-ed.*

*The peo-ple, uni-ted,*
*will ne-ver be de-feat-ed.*

Chico Mendes, what a Hero,
What an energy of protest he did create,
They thought they killed Chico's campaign
When they murdered him, but instead
They created thousands of Chico Mendeses around the world,
And don't you know you can't kill energy,
It just transfers to another state.

*The peo-ple, uni-ted,*
*will ne-ver be de-feat-ed.*

*The peo-ple, uni-ted,*
*will ne-ver be de-feat-ed.*

*The peo-ple, uni-ted,*
*will ne-ver be de-feat-ed.*

Viva la spirito de Chico Mendes.
Long live the spirit of Chico Mendes.

## Total Extinction

*Courtesy of an Excessive Consumer Society*

Do you love earth and realise its worth?

Earth's temperature rising like huge blue flames;
Earth has fed you and lunged you since birth,
The polar ice caps are melting in vain.

Earth's temperature rose like huge blue flames,
Giant demon waves consume towns and cities;
The young and the old;
The polar ice caps have melted in vain,
Environmental disasters make the earth erode.

Giant demon waves consumed towns and cities;
The young and the old,
Tsunamis, tornados, forest fires and floods;
Environmental disasters made the earth erode,
Fatal heat waves and droughts drain earth's life blood.

Tsunamis, tornados, forest fires and floods,
Earth fed you and lunged you since birth;
Fatal heat waves and droughts drained earth's life blood.

Did you love earth and realise its worth?

The theory of big bang was birthed by a catholic priest,
Like air I am omnipresent,
The priest was Lemaitre - he wasn't an Atheist,
Like sun burning I am omnipotent.

Like air I am omnipresent,
I am the universe the dark energy,
Like sun burning I am omnipotent,
I'm the hands you call gravity.

I am the universe the dark energy,
Guardians watch over you - the white winged messengers,
I'm the hands you call gravity,
I work from a laboratory near the planet Vega.

Guardians watch over you - the white winged messengers,
The priest was Lemaitre - he wasn't an Atheist,
I work from a laboratory near the planet Vega,
The theory of big bang was birthed by a catholic priest.

We are a big family,
We live on the ground,
But we don't make a sound.
We have seeds, stem and leaves,
And we sometimes grow on trees.
We have many names,
But we don't play games.
We create spices for your food,
Fruit for cakes and ice cream,
And herbs for your mood,
Leaves for your tea,
And beans for your coffee,
Cane for your sugar,
And flowers for your mother,
Wheat for your bread,
And medicine for your head,
Cocoa for your chocolate
And cotton for your clothes,
Fragrances for perfume
Like Lavender and rose.
Although you see us in the supermarket
In packages with labels,
We're there because we were planted,
So don't take us for granted,
We are the family of plants.

## Crystal Clear

We began as mountains
And ended up as rocks,
You can dig for us at quarries
Or buy us in shops.
We've lived here since the dawn of time
So we're very old,
We're hard, strong and solid,
We're hot and we're cold.
We're in many colours, shapes and sizes,
And we have many names,
We're all individuals, and yet
We're all the same.
We were born in nature's garden,
But over time we will harden.
We are Rose, Clear and Smoky quartz,
We are Blue Lace Agate,
We are Sodalite,
We are Malachite,
We are Aventurine and Citrine.
We see Angels in the Rainbow,
And Demons in the Volcano.
We hear, Crystal Clear,
Thunder clapping,
Wind howling,
Waves lapping.
We began as mountains,
And ended up as rocks.

I used to live at Rock Bottom,
But now I'm closer to the Peak,
Don't think that because I'm white
I've had an easy life,
Part English, Irish, Welsh and Jewish,
There's no such thing as a perfect race,
Everyone is mixed you will find if you trace
Back your roots far enough,
Pure Blood is the Imperialist's Bluff
They use to maintain power over us,
Flags and skin colour and forms that want
To see specifics of ethnicity,
If it doesn't matter then why don't they leave it
Until the Interview to ask you?
A superiority complex is a facade wall
Built to hide vulnerability,
With a know it all attitude,
Inflated ego and words,
To put down your views if different from theirs,
By being unkind by saying your mind
Is susceptible to simplistic beliefs,
The Truth is that no-one really knows Anything,
We just choose which theories and things to believe,
So Creationist or Evolutionist
Unless you can give me a guarantee,
You can't dismiss my beliefs or me.

"These honest, raw and uncompromising protest poems, a blistering cocktail of the personal, political, cultural and environmental goad, provoke and compel us into reflection. Autobiographical yet traversing private borders they transport us into worlds both alien yet starkly familiar."

*Terry Hughes*
*Edinburgh Fringe First award-winning playwright*


"A collection of hard-hitting verses. The title of the opening poem, 'Bipolar - Type II', introduces the theme of disorder - particularly in thinking. Returning back to childhood, "All sights, smells and sounds" are intensified, "filling" the poet back up. It appears that there is something missing and absent within the chaos. "Anything is possible" and the poet grows "restless" and panicked. The world is viewed in a "new way". Readers will be thrown into the middle of a chaos which they cannot escape. The first poem characterises those that follow. All are trapped within the subject of conflict. Poems pivot around flashbacks, past events or current chaos. In 'Chained' an unhealthy attachment - or "chaining" - to an abusive lover is explored. The subject matter grows political and critical of war and austerity in poems such as 'Austerity is a Lie'. 'Refugees of World War III' observes the Syrian refugee crisis. *Order & Chaos* is fantastically reflective of chaos whilst calling for order."

*The Nubian Times*

"The biographical nature of Julia Davenport's poems makes the printed words on the page become raw and alive, rich in emotion and memory that engages all of the reader's senses. Davenport is the under-dog whose words have a bite, the final line in her section well sums up her key message "You can't dismiss my beliefs or me" ['Outside the Box']. These are poems for today that need not only to be heard but to be acted upon - NOW!"

*Naomi Sumner Chan*
*Creative Director at Brush Stroke Order*

"This is strong work, full of life and energy. At times angry and uncompromising, especially when political, it is unapologetically polemic at times. There are poetic techniques employed, mainly rhythm, repetition and strong imagery, that beat out like a chant or a protest song, filled with force and fire. Julia asks, about the Manchester Ship Canal: "What would you do with 330,000 litres of water?" Later in the same poem she says, "Look out for the shadows and ghosts of men and horses / Who towed canal boats.". Above all this is poetry that cares, about people, about culture, and about the environment. As such, it is unforgettable. As such, it needs to be read and heard."

*Cathy Bryant*
*ed. Best of Manchester Poets, vols. 1-3*

42904277R00034

Printed in Poland
by Amazon Fulfillment
Poland Sp. z o.o., Wrocław